ALONE IN THE HOUSE OF MY HEART

ALSO BY KARI GUNTER-SEYMOUR

A Place So Deep Inside America It Can't Be Seen

Serving (chapbook)

Alone in the House of My Heart

Poems

KARI GUNTER-SEYMOUR

SWALLOW PRESS

ATHENS, OHIO

Swallow Press
An imprint of Ohio University Press, Athens, Ohio 45701
ohioswallow.com

Printed in the United States of America
Swallow Press / Ohio University Press books are printed
on acid-free paper ∞ ™

30 29 28 27 26 25 24 23 22   5 4 3 2 1

Library of Congress Cataloging-in-Publication Data
Names: Gunter-Seymour, Kari, author.
Title: Alone in the house of my heart : poems / Kari Gunter-Seymour.
Description: Athens, Ohio : Swallow Press, [2022]
Identifiers: LCCN 2022028048 (print) | LCCN 2022028049
  (ebook) | ISBN 9780804012430 (paperback ; acid-free paper) |
  ISBN 9780804041232 (pdf)
Subjects: LCGFT: Poetry.
Classification: LCC PS3607.U54818 A79 2022 (print) | LCC
  PS3607.U54818 (ebook) | DDC 811/.6—dc23/eng/20220613
LC record available at https://lccn.loc.gov/2022028048
LC ebook record available at https://lccn.loc.gov/2022028049

For my people—

steeped in survival and hallelujah

CONTENTS

One

Two

Five

One

The light on the wall
holds all I know.

I've been thinking about last times
I never knew were the last—
Grandma cooing me unconscious,
Daddy whistling me home to supper,
my toddler's toothless grin, tiny fingers
clenching wildflowers, the last time
I prayed, desperate for those departed,
how they flit ahead of us, flying.

Tonight the Big Dipper balances
on its handle. Tepid tree frogs peep
songs of resurrection. One morning soon,
I'll eat a good breakfast, fill a water bottle,
pack a book, walk the fencerow into the holler,
rest beneath the eagle's favored perch,
shake off this inexplicable sadness,
two cinderblocks where lungs ought to be,
let spring hold on to me for a while.

When she was a teen, a baby
wriggled from my mother's arms,
hit the ground hard. She told no one
but me, shortly before her death.
Too late to bring peace to anyone
but herself. Now I'm stuck
completing her sentence.

If you could see my words,
splattered, a serif typeface,
magnified by one thousand,
you might understand
how ragged I am.

At the center of me—this crater
of me—I wrestle with my tendency
to take on ruined energy.
Everything hidden is pluckable,
given time—tender shoots
in matter-of-fact tones,
roiling helter-skelter from the tongue,
echoing like a gunshot through the heart.

I wake with the same weird
hairdo my cat wakes up with,
squeeze my eyes until stars
swirl, hope to make my body
be anywhere but here, all sallow
cheeks and blood memory.

The thinning feathers of her eyelashes,
scant scar on the bridge of her nose,
tongue compelling her lips—
harsh as a sip of halfpenny gin, the hiss,
the spitting out of something too strong.

Sunday morning, the alarm set
for dawn, I gargle lemon water
to loosen phlegm, open vocal cords.
Mother, postured at the piano, paces me
up and down the major scales,
Are you washed in the blood of the Lamb?

I dress in a starched white blouse,
an A-line skirt hemmed precisely
below the knee. Mother stands behind me
in the mirror—cat-eye glasses, Pentecostal bun,
hot-curls my ragged mane into
a semblance of respectable.

Later, in the choir loft, Mother leans,
her coffee breath all over me,
whispers loud enough
for the soprano section to hear,
You're too pretty to be so fat.

You won't remember all he did
to you, evidence notwithstanding,
tawny eyelashes and pale arms suffocated
in shadow, strips of your skin curled away,
your body a vessel, spilled, then filled
with ash, a window overlooking
your ruin a part of the illusion.

There will be moments—reminders,
the awful music of salacious syllables
crackling the air, the heat compelling
your body to shrink, gasp for breath,
lungs spilled then filled with contradiction.
Look back far enough, it all becomes
suppressible, a drawerful of rubble and grit.

An aura surrounds you, chafes
the alabaster walls, which has nothing to do
with transformation and everything
to do with speculation, the future not what
it used to be, spilled, then filled with soot.
Your face, now merely a suggestion
of your face, poised, ready to blow
out a match, held to your lips,
your mouth desperate with teeth.

If my name were an animal,
it would be brown dog, dreaming
of squirrels to hound, near-empty
dinner plates, buried bone maps,
the certainty of trees.

If a spice it would be fennel,
musty after rain, drops swelling
the bud-point of every bough,
a murmuration of starlings
circling clouds.

If my name were a spirit,
it would be barrel-aged,
laughter laced in undertones
of honey, fig, and citrus,
the burden for truth unfettered.

If a color? The hour before
a thunderstorm, a cerulean warbler
or stalwart stalks of chicory,
jagged petals wagging
their tongues in waves.

If my name were music,
it would be the *hur-uff* of a doe,
hoof deep in acorns and orange-
gold leaves, the cicadas
calling me *home, home, home*

When you were a boy, I whispered
tangled yarns, swore they cobbled stars
into shapes. Faces moonward we hooted,
Dipper, Dragon, Archer, Crab.

You, scant as an eggling fallen from
its nest. I trip-wired, full of excuses
and stacks of put-off things, pages where
words of bliss or angst were strewn.

Outside my window a suckling fawn
stands moonstruck—spindly legged,
freckled fur, shadow stretched, confused,
its tears a trick of the light.

Without warning, the bane of my being
sends me a text about a four-inch-long scratch
on my toddler grandson's arm, one that,
swear to God, he already had when
he arrived for our last visit.

I know she is trying to set my son up,
document false evidence so he will lose
privileges or the right to see his fragile boy,
who runs on all fours, hides in the dog's crate
the minute anyone sets foot inside the house.

When I think of her, this young woman,
obviously lonely, who wanted to get married—
a sharp-edged prickle inside my head
repeats, *Beware!*

She started sleeping with crystals,
my son says, scratching his head—
I mean actual rocks in our bed.

On nights I drink too much wine
I blame myself—my A-line skirts,
Weight Watchers diets,
my son growing up single-mommed
inside small-town America,

lured off course by a spritz
of patchouli, a flash of black lace.

Tonight I weep for all I cannot fix,
wish for a newfangled deity to implore,
a *let's make a deal* beyond altar and incense,
a clearinghouse for the backlog of karma.

I drape a makeshift veil over my head,
one hand raised in supplication,
the other shielding my heart.

I could not manage the gloves,
chunk after chunk, fresh-split firewood,
that sliver sliding in unnoticed,
but for a tiny tingle,
in the struggle to keep up.

It was not to be needled or tweezed,
besting me from all sides,
my face pinched
in concentration, sweat,
setting myself down
on the wood-planked floor.

I daydream the beach,
your tiny boy legs brown,
sand stamped, face striped with sun.
I choke on clouds, thrown forward,
your assault rifle cocked,
cradled in the crook of your arm.

Shrapnel, pinpricks gray and blue
dot your cheek and brow,
hollow pain that cannot save.
The numb sodality of death
festers, fills your head with cruel grace,
your memories impossibly wide.

Light makes the whole place look queer,
angles and shadows, sky dark,
ratcheting everything down.
Tops of the oaks toss back and forth,
clacking their branches together.

Behind them a rumbling.
Thunder? Someone's truck gearing
down to take the hill,
life somehow slipping out of gear.

I taught you to dream this yard in Ohio
where the grass holds the shapes of your feet,
where clouds are the breaths of trees,
the wind their voices.

Prayed it would ward you,
the blood and bone smell of it,
overthrowing the hiss in your head.
They can say anything, do anything,
bring anything out at any moment,
hope to do you in.

You will have spring rain,
the tin roof, the windowsill,
the smell of fresh baked bread,
your rascally black dog
haunched and cockeyed,
waiting by the mailbox.

Sleepless, I huddled in a rocker
on the back porch, jacket zipped,
hood up, invisible—or so I thought,
inside the shadow of a full Milk Moon.

She crossed just shy of the tall grass,
twenty feet in front of me, lit up
in creamy glow—dark spotted, huge feet
heaving her up the weedy bank to the edge
of the woods, ear tufts suddenly alert,
head swiveling over her shoulder.

I have seen that look before, in a photograph
of my great-grandmother—a woman
stalked and caught. I have imagined her
screech in the night, my own throat
suddenly airless, the hairs on the back
of my neck stinging, the cat ricocheting
through the pines, gone.

Two

Oh, spittle-pale blossom,
the tree is done with you.

Whatever it was that held mother together
all these years, is unraveling like a daytime soap opera—
turned out like the dusk of her underbed,
pacing the kitchen, hands churning air,
as if word for word was the same as moment by moment,
repetition the answer to prayer.

During the Great War, electricity was used as cure.
Volts routed through fractured cerebellums,
or directly on sectors of the body where derangements
were manifest. Those enduring matters of the heart
often undone by the overzealous.

Cracked as a broken mirror and all its mess,
her hours decline to halves, halves to minutes,
an empty frame all that remains
of the what, the where, or the not of her.

OHIO STRUGGLES TO CONTAIN
COVID-19 NURSING HOME DEATHS

It's Tuesday and if the world
had not splintered,
I would be driving into town
as I have every other.

My mother, gone thin some
months ago, sits locked away,

trapped between memory
and the moment, her body rusting.

Other daughters hold her now,
masked, silvering threads of life
cradled in their latexed hands.

March winds blow biting
against a gray cloudless day.
I cover my mouth, hunker down.

How far across the sky will this Corona
spread its doom?

Give her stiff white sheets flapping the line,
cloud-etched, like when she was a girl,
the tang of weeping cherry undermining
the bleach, a brood of plucky banties
in the barnyard, crickets stitching the afternoon.

Pardon her reflection, the silvery
sheen of her thinning hair, twiglike fingers
gripping the sill, cheekbones wan
in afternoon light, eyes round as coins
placed on the dead.

Leave her the names of her two children,
the smell of woodsmoke, acres of sunflowers,
the climb east up the mountain,
my palm pressed flat against the pane,
our breaths fogging the glass.

Spare her the torment, the sick
and dying, falling like raindrops
on freshly turned soil.

The conversation began
with a false step, everything
that followed was a downward
plunge, the silence left
in the middle of a sentence.

Said she felt like she was—
what was the word?
Only to realize it was one
of the first she'd learned,
one of her earliest memories.

After that, to know
it could happen again,
did happen, everything transient,
leaving her like her child self,
struggling to fill the gap.

Elsewhere, people wake,
make coffee, listen to the news.
She is focused on the process
of loss, dropping dead words
into private conversations.

As if somewhere in the mix,
she might find an end
to the mortification,
or just one day the voice
inside her head does not judge.

Scolding your husband
for an empty coffee pot,
your mother for dying, your son
for being a drunk, even as
he celebrates one year sober,
stashing your own liquor bottles
deep inside the dirty-clothes hamper.

I lie fetal inside
the Statue of Liberty's torch,
the one removed in 1984,
now displayed in the lobby,

 its warped copper frame
 a coiled energy about to unwind,
 swoop like a wood thrush.

I was not the daughter
my mother needed.
She often warned,
Lord, don't never have children.

 Aren't all of us born to be
 the receptacle of our parent's flame,
 God the most popular protagonist?

Like the Lady, my mama was
most beautiful in sunlight,
puckered apron, trowel in one hand,
Bible raised in the other, tired, poor.

She kept a clean house, grew
collards and heirloom tomatoes
strapped to stakes like sinners
begging the lash, sewed

all my clothes, a wisp of prayer
with every up/down of the needle,
trusting one day her willful daughter
would fettle herself out.

Heeled under my mother's eyes,
the smudge of every lusterless day
she endured.

This dream?
A wood thrush taking wing,
tittering,
Too late, too late.

Today I paid a man to plant a tree
in honor of my mother,
compelled by sentiment and the idea
of restoration, as in habitat
for rare Kirtland warblers, who
are picky, require jack pines
rooted in Grayling sand.

My mother was a rare bird,
colorful, flighty, could trill
a rich, clear aria.
She never left the house without
her signature kohled eyelids
and some form of feather-crested frock.
Given the chance, she, too, would
have wintered in the Bahamas.

Side-eyed, she would scoff
at hard-earned cash spent to hire a man
to plant a tree, in sand no less,
in the next breath insist on hiring a woman
to nurture its growth.

One day soft breezes will fluff her
slender branches, her ruffled needles
thrumming a chorus of hatchling lullabies.
The land, the woods, the preak,
pruck, purr of all wild creatures,
mist pearling the pines.

Already the sumac—ripened,
rusty-red leaves stark among the greens.
Not yet, I say. I say it every August,
though leafy lime katydids warn me,
chameleoned against the Japanese maples,
suddenly outsinging even the cicadas.
Stink bugs feast in the garden, a melancholy
thistle bends to a rumor of breeze.

The alcohol has stopped working.
My anger has become an affliction
I work hard to dial down, like
an election cycle or tuba solo.

So much to be controlled,
everything languaged to death,
the backstory of our cherished
whittled down to a spreadsheet.
All the desperate utterances we tweet
to be superficially soothed,
our reward a scattering of posts
and heart-shaped clicks.

What is history anyway,
but a conversation we're born into
without context, a string of songs
about heartbreak, a universe
that made us from its shattering and dust?
Some days you're handling the grief,
others, you're a dog in a car doing donuts
in a Walmart parking lot.

Everything has a dream of itself.
The world rewards those tailored
to its patterns, the rest left naked to fend.
Birds are loudest just before daybreak.

Every morning they sing, all brass
and woodwind, convinced they bring the light.

Even tapered, my anger leans in,
holds me anchored, sifting through endless
memes and search engines, abandoned
glassware, melting ice, sweat rings,
the stench of bitterness and booze.

Midnight seeps the cracks.
I cannot for the life of me conjure
the scent of hay, spicy sweet,
stacked high inside the barn before frost.

I suspect my nesting place is still there,
sunbeams slanting the loft.
Some other father tending the tractor,
some other mother baking cornbread,
frying bacon to flavor the beans.
Some other daughter who prefers
Sylvia Plath and dusty brown sheep.

I've spent the day staring down
this blank page, bones on fire,
wrung out so dry I can't siphon a tear.
How many words, dressed in apologies
and alibis, to represent a life,
at twenty-five cents each?

In the space between sighs, walls fade
to meadow, a cotton-cloud sky.
Mother's breaths are scant and labored.
I kiss her forehead, tuck a wayward curl,
sing the way of morning birds, deep and throaty,
leave her resting on a bed of wildflowers,
hayfields swaying tawny in the sun.

No exaggeration, an entire field filled—
daffodils, golden heads bobbing. Took her years
to divide and transplant the bulbs, gently
scooping under each clump, every nub a new life,
fragrant, a mingling of earth's brine
and spice, the way a newborn smells.

Bronzed and shapely, she'd planted
herself midway, one casually laced boot
in front of the other, morning sun defining
her contours. When she lifted her arms,
cowbirds took to the sky like nymphs
of cool breezes and she their Terra Gaia.

I framed the photo, pearls of sweat
frosting her upper lip, but not before
she wrote near the bottom
in careful cursive—
Below my feet my child sleeps.

Three

Low clouds kissing whatever they find,
every splinter spoken for.

Daddy didn't like watermelon,
he loved cantaloupe, *muskmelon*,
our family called it. He would
cut one in half, scrape the seeds,
add a shake of salt inside the cavity, feast.

Daddy and his people grew up
in Putnam County, barefoot, feral.
He declared cantaloupes grown
along the East Fork Obey River,
where the air sweats and melons
swell like teats on a bluetick,
the best on earth.

Every year, late July, our family
made the pilgrimage. He'd sniff
and thump, roll them over,
looking for blanched spots
on their netted rinds, evidence
of ripening in the field.
Like all best things, they didn't last long.

Come midsummer, I'll make my way
to Putnam County. In spirit, my daddy
will ride shotgun, shirt sleeves rolled,
collar open, puffing a Parliament Menthol
as I speed down old Highway 53, mouth watering,
the bottomlands calling me home.

My father was a kind man who survived
into his seventies, but died at the age
of eighteen, on a tiny atoll in the Pacific,
when Japanese forces finally failed and he,
one of the lucky ones, returned to the States
bleeding memories as the nation cheered
and squirreled away savings bonds.
Even today body bags are cheap.

Facebook rants—politics, race,
sexual orientation. Clean-cut white boys
wear red ball caps, carry torches.
Elsewhere skeletal babies bat at flies,
distended bellies evidence
of their expendability, while would-be
do-gooders throw fundraising galas,
cocktail their way to martyrdom.

I've had a few brews, a good soup,
the diner's south-facing window
bronzed and full blooded.
I'm reflecting on how light arranges itself
no matter the circumstance,
how childhood teaches us
to covet shiny things.

How we carry our baggage—
judgment easy, knowledge difficult.

And though I want it to be so,
not everything can be blamed
on ignorance or pride.

The waiter gives me *the look*,
table clear but for a spoon,
refracting, jewel-like.
I want another beer, but won't ask,
the room gone cold, but the light,
my God, the light.

We might should blame Eve,
or that rascal Newton.
But I say it was Gessler, bastard,
though who could have known
what would come of his vengeance—
Tell's defiance, his son's famous stance?

This perfectly delicious one,
grievously balanced, shadow shaped.
Cloud guts, pithy and sweet, spewed
insides out, beyond freckled skin,
shards and debris making slick work
of that steel, that lead, spinning fast and true.

That silly boys would forever
set one to head, aim whatever,
egged on by the romance of muscle
and munitions. Killing fruit, then birds,
then animals, then each other.

Problem was, she felt too much
or not at all, a practiced yearning
that had no name. Her kids grown,
gone, forty years behind her,
fields rutted, shutters listless,
the barn propped and cockeyed.
All those young bride prayers wasted.

Creatures like sheep, used to traveling,
know about moving on, guided by
the compass of their will, boredom
an affliction that can't be outrun, desire
a grassy knob worth dying for. How
utterly a body is overruled by heartache.

Outside red oaks thrash, tangled
in root and bird song and whatever
might fall from the sky.
Her last undoing was to set her sassy
banties free to peck and roam,
scratch out a destiny of their own.

Your great-grandfather worked this land fifty years.
A church-going man, fit and leathery, thickest
arms I ever saw. He often *took a spell,*
like his father before him, aggravated by change
of season, kept tolerable by great-grand's threats
of abdication, and late-night sips of Applejack.
He took his leave of farming at seventy,
firm of belly, back plumb as a disc blade.
Left us a year later, overcome by boredom, fast food,
and a paralyzing sense of doom neither fuss
nor poultice could harness.

Your dad's dad was a factory man.
He *suffered a moodiness* and excesses of light.
Thirty years, eight-hour shifts,
followed nightly by longneck bottles,
served ice cold at Louie's Bar & Grill.
He was the quiet one, a sipper,
until the day libation failed him.
Swamped by light, his demons no longer soothed,
he took ghastly pleasure in revealing secrets
accumulated over years of stillness and wily observation.

Through the parlor window, we watch rain
drift in waves across the river's choppy rise.
Lightning splits the sky, the weight of air thins.
A dustup of wind whirls pockets of scent
heady with promise. Promise the garden will thrive,
the thirsty Ohio will hold its drink, and the Zoloft
prescribed by the clinic will banish the spirits.

Today I gave a guy a ride,
caught in a cloudburst
jogging down East Mill Street.
Skinny, backpacked, newspaper
a makeshift shield, unsafe
under any circumstances.
I don't know what possessed me.

I make bad decisions, am forgetful,
cling to structure and routine
like static electricity to polyester,
a predicament of living under
the facade I always add to myself.

Said he needed to catch a GoBus,
shaking off droplets before climbing in.
He gabbed about Thanksgiving plans,
his mom's cider-basted turkey,
grandma's pecan-crusted pumpkin pie.

It was a quick masked ride.
Bless you, he said, unfolding himself
from the car. No awkward goodbyes,
no what do I owe you? Just *Bless you*
and a backward wave.

At the stop sign, my fingers stroked
the dampness where he sat minutes before.

Sometimes life embraces you
so unconditionally, it shifts
your body from shadow
into a full-flung lotus of light.

Rollerblader, unsung crusader,
champion of feral dogs and crippled cats.

Cake baker, sleep faker, you once dressed
as a girl for Halloween because

you wanted to feel firsthand,
how difficult that life might be.

We did what we could,
hid the bottles, drove what
was left of him deep
into the yawning hollow,
built a campfire, drank water
from a long-handled gourd,
a galvanized bucket.

We set up tents for triage,
counted his breaths, worried
over irregular heartbeats,
sweats, persistent vomiting,
his jacked-up adrenal system.

We waited. Listened for a canvas
zipper in the night, each long, slow
pull a call to duty, our legs folding
over duct-taped camp stools,
tucked tight around the fire,
his gut-fucked stories, stenched
in blood and munitions,
overpowering the woodsmoke's
curling carbons.

Crows haunched on branches
behind our backs, sentinels,
silent as we wept.

We doused him in creek water,
a sharp sheen of moon over our bones,
recited communions, sang songs
our mothers taught us in the womb,
every neighbor dog and coyote
within earshot barking hill to valley.

Some people think they
don't deserve to be loved,
every story scratched
into the dirt an ache.
That week, down in the lower forty
we all got born again.
It was hard to say who saved who.

Wayside bar, pitchers of beer,
couple lines of coke out back.
Why she come home after
all those years was never made clear.
Feet bare, voice like water pulled
from a well, mouth urgent
for the sound of her own name.

He, our beautiful loser, laid-back
and impulsive, says all the right words.
Says he wants her dirty, sweat
and grit, mind-your-mouth dirty.
Wants her the way a river bends.

For weeks they tangle,
far-flung, reckless.
We watch their muscles move
under tight skin, his flame,
her moist cooing.
Two names scrawled in bark,
her laughter the long shadow
that will follow him for years,
none of us sober long enough
to recognize all she was capable of.

What's left of him quivers
in the rearview—

tell a lie long enough,
it will become the truth.
We round our empty mouths to say it.

Belly up, you beautiful thing, strong legged
and twang drawled, raised holler to mountain top,
rich in root, fed on lard biscuits and bacon gravy.

Lick at the longnecked bottle, your tongue
a divination, your face a fist, two sweat-moons
where breasts ache to swing and sway.

Unclasp those bindings and all who contrive them,
their straps and underwires camouflaged in curlicues,
icy hands groping, the pitiful way you must offer
bits of your body, your land, to earn so little
as a pine-splint stool at their stars-and-stripes table.

Drink to the twisted torch of freedom, washed down
with fracking waste, red clay dust, the bitter soot
of coal's *see ya later sucka!* Say, *Hell yes*,
to the crack and splinter of misogynist pulpits.

Give rise your manifesto, each word
draping the bud-point of every bough,
your body never again obliged, your song
a rush of wings, like souls releasing.

The winds tonight could be beautiful
if they didn't feel so rawboned.
I watch the yard shift, spring blooms
ripped from stems, bodiless wings,
mangled chroma littering the grass,
the creek burbling.

I'm toting a notebook,
a stray felt-tip pen, pink ink.
Scraps of verse ride climbing currents.
I take them as they come,
consider failures, margins of loss,
each word a blush.

Soon rain will muscle its way,
insist on its place. I will run,
fawn fleet in the pale leaf light,
notebook a slipshod shelter,
pray none of the bones
the creek spits up will be mine.

Sunday afternoon. Taylor Swift's latest nonsense
caterwauls on the radio, a third-string agitation,
compared to my son trying to bootlick his daughter
into jumping in our pond off the high dive,
nine feet up a steep planked ladder.

A pinch of a girl, she just this week turned six
and I wonder where that rascal in him comes from.
I blame his father, long gone and good riddance.
My true husband, a gem, who knows me all too well,
taps his sandaled foot against my pinky toe,
slightly shakes his head, because my granddaughter
just cold-shouldered her daddy, ran to fetch
her fishing pole instead.

Though I don't want it, those twelve soccer boys,
clear the other side of the world, are on my mind.
Trapped miles inside a cave, tides rising, huddled
and hungry, licking water drops from crusty walls.
Last week, Navy SEALs rose from the depths
like apparitions, brought pep talks, promises,
concocting on the fly, ways those boys, who don't
even know how to swim, could strap on a face mask,
practice a few strokes, MacGyver their way free.

We cool ourselves in the water, ride four-wheelers,
reach for icy Coca-Colas, popsicles, slices of melon.

We're fixing to pack it in when breaking
news blasts the radio. *Christ almighty,*
four of those boys made it out, others
not far behind, SEALs at their backs, urging.

Soon after, my wily son afloat below the dive,
that plucky grandbaby of mine sets down her pole,
climbs the ladder, leaps like a fish-nymph,
hoots as she breaks the surface.

I am never happy to see summer go,
earth stripped of its finest voice.
I am sitting outside in my heavy coat,
porch light off. There is no moon,
no ambient distractions, the sky a Zion.

I take solace in considering the age
of this valley, the way water
left its mark on Appalachia,
long before Peabody sunk a shaft,
Chevron augured the shale, or ODOT
dynamited roadways through steep rock.

I grew up in a house where canned
fruit cocktail was considered a treat.
My sister and I fought over who got
to eat the fake cherries, standouts in the can,
though tasting exactly like every other
tired piece of fruit floating in the heavy syrup.

But it was store-bought, like city folks',
and we were too gullible to understand
the corruption in the concept, our mother's
home-canned harvests superior in every way.
I cringe when I think of how we shamed her.

So much here depends upon
a green corn stalk, a patched barn roof,

weather, the Lord, community.
We've rarely been offered a hand
that didn't destroy.

Inside the house the lightbulb comes on
when the refrigerator door is opened.
My husband rummages a snack,
plops beside me on the porch to wolf it down,
turns, plants a kiss, leans back in his chair,
says to no one in particular,
A person could spend a lifetime
under a sky such as this.

To all loose limbed and weary,
set aside your relationship

with windows and doors.
Orphan your woes.

Cross over the sedum,
the woolly thyme,

ease the embankment.
Minnows dart,

starlings rise and dip,
foothills glaze the sun.

Listen—

birdlings tweep, deer *hur-uff*,
silver maples thrum.

Dragonflies, lizards, monarchs, bees,
Come rest, they say,

lay open your sack of troubles
to the sky.

Four

Mostly, a cage is air.

Our baptism was near at hand, the creeks
brimming with spring rain, yellow crocus
poking up their heads with suspicion.
We wiggled in our seats all through May.

That summer Knobs got her nickname,
being the first of us who, when chin
was put to chest, could barely see her toes.
She flaunted her stardom floating on her back.

We frittered our way to Labor Day
worrying nibs of straw between our teeth,
vowing never to smoke or drink or carry on
with men outside the church.

To this day I will swear
Wanda Sue Banks was our undoing.
Her lanky self, strutting into our lives,
eyelashes thick with Maybelline.
She popped her gum, stole her
mama's cigarettes, and we were
drawn to her like flies to dog doo.

She collected us.
We teased our hair, kohled our eyelids,
turned up our hemlines with duct tape.
She taught us the power of moodiness.

We were fixing to joyride in her daddy's Fairlane
the day our mothers grabbed us by the arm.

Years later I read about her in the newspaper
and cried, Ultra Big Lash Mascara smudging
my hanky and cheeks.

I was thirteen, she was Barbie—
tight waisted, pointy ta-tas,
teensy purple pom-poms glued
to sexy high-heeled slings.
Ken and Madge, a glamorous
seaside life splashed on the cover
of every teen magazine
in the A&P Food Store checkout line.

I come from farm folk, short, stocky,
built to dig a ditch, throw a bale.
My mother bargained:
lose five pounds, earn Barbie.

Life blurred into a ragged routine—
beef patties, cottage cheese,
running the path from the barn
to the woods. I passed out during
gym class, my teacher furious to learn
of my mother's arrangement.

Barbie came to me pasty pale, pouty
lipped, nose pugged, in a stretchy
strapless striped swimsuit that provoked
the pink in my daddy's cheeks.

No crease or fold, no nest of pubic wonder,
she could not stand, her arches cruelly

vaulted, gravity and her ginormous
chesties faceplanting her without fail.

She could not manage her white plastic
sunglasses or floppy flowered hat,
her quarter-sized woven wicker beach bag
forever slipping off her rock-hard
plastic shoulder. One attempt to comb
her sun-streaked coif and off popped
her vacant head.

Come haying season, I lost five pounds
throwing bales good as any of the boys.
My new obsession? To insist
ordinary things be somehow more—
a brittle leaf laced in snow,
the sugary smell of clover-filled pastures,
my mother's voice, twanged and weedy,
calling, *Don't be late for supper!*

Skink:

My first had scales// a lanky body, protracted tail// angular bones in arms and legs// her Barbie-sized finger-claws// to be seen only up close// which was hardly ever// She was a darter// between cracks in the hedge wall// the base of the barn's foundation// or lolling, belly to ground in the shadows// *You are the dreamer of your life,* she intimated ad nauseam// Red throated and five-lined// one eye on her target, the other on the cosmos// I once saw her cry from her third eye// crunching her way through a cricket// (someone else's adviser)// who thrashed its hindlegs// between her teensy bladed teeth// his clickity-clackity forever kaput// One day losing patience, I lunged for her// ruddy tail tip pinched between my fingers// her badass-self gone, girl, gone// her cosmic consciousness spouting, *Let that be your lesson*//

Tortoise:

The next I never loved// her constant cowardice// knobby, gnarled neck shrinking into carapace//at the slightest mention of my obsessions// bad men, good booze, iffy pharmaceuticals// I tired of her dullness, her flat feet// her old-goddess energy// her constant nagging *slow down, slow down*// her yak, yak, yak, duty to carry mother earth, yada, yada// thirteen moons segmenting her dorsum// always showing up for the worst of me// The day I found her on her back// puny legs flailing// I laughed so hard I cried//

Hawk:

My last one broke me// his broad chest, his buteo chassis// the coppered bronze of each pinion's edge// His conspicuously curled claws// the hook of his rock-hard bill// his stomach-lurching Kamikaze spirals, groundward//

seconds before pulling out// the lusty residue of carnage and musk prickling my tongue// I pouted his pontifical speeches// *drama queen!*// applauded his soaring circles// my eyes cloud-soaked// body breathless, ground-bound// an ogler demanding attention// refusing his omens// the colors of death// The morning he quit me// the breeze felt like a balm// but was in fact that high-speed updraft of air// just before the talon slashes//

I wake to flat hair.
The tug of time spidering
across my reflection,
tightening over my
forehead's bone.

Beyond the drafty glass
sit yellowed fields
and ruined gardens.
A lone bird pecks
at some once-seeded thing.

I am a brittle leaf
trapped against a wire fence,
a trickle of rusty water
teasing like the sense
of something waiting to unfold,

leaving only the wait.

Poetry the way he entered the world,
he uncoiled casually, stumping
how deeply his roots were fixed:
Some are born a willow, some an oak,
arms overhead to demonstrate
how trees flex their bodies.

We raced motorcycles, camped hollers,
skinny-dipped quarries, spit
watermelon seeds, snitched cigarettes
and hits off his daddy's Jim Beam bottles.

He grew to favor throaty blues,
flask in his pocket, joint behind his ear,
Oxy and Vikes, *just for fun,*
his laughter addictive, women
all ages loved his bad ass.

This morning brittle branches spike
jagged shadows across his neglected lawn,
the sky bruised like a drug-addled vein.
I cock my head, wait for some
perfect sound, the silence so heavy
cicadas pause their keening.

Unlike your ex-husband, Buzz
never sought the favor of other women
or left you alone when you cried.
He was quick to bite or otherwise
scare the sweet Jesus out of trespassers,
dashing out the garage door
when your children paid a visit,
yipping and carrying on,
his crack-the-whip tail bashing
flowerpots and unguarded knees.

You called me from your cell phone
speaking like a woman possessed.
Between sobs I heard
Damn it, shit. Bring a gun.
I packed pain pills
and a bottle of wine instead.

Howls, wretched and humanlike,
echoed down your drive. I jogged
the trail to the side yard, air thick
with honeysuckle and humidity.

He dragged his hindquarters desperate
to rise, eyes dark, begging release.
Crushing pills in the pestle, I concocted

what I hoped was a paralyzing potion.
We sipped the Malbec and cried.

Rose and gray streaked the sky
when a pistol at last did come,
in the steady hands of a knowing farmer.
Your boys dug the grave.
Crickets chirped the seconds
as each of us in turn paid our last respects.

Driving home in the dark,
fireflies caroused in the fields,
flickering like mad,
as if it might be their last chance.

I want to scribble lines about
the bluebird duo pecking, pecking
at my morning window,
a'flap like wrung-out hummingbirds,
chittering as if the place were on fire.

Google tells me bluebirds are at great
risk of predation, highly vulnerable
even inside their nesting box,
which must be fortified just so.

I want to wax on about
how the male's blue-black wings
and blood-orange throat
make him stand out markedly
against the affluent green
of spring, compared to the pallidness
of his missus and myself.

I don't want to write about
George Floyd or the shadow
that blocked the sky,
at his throat nine minutes, a pasty-pale
punk with a badge, kneeling
him to death, while our man
begs *please*,
        Officer, I can't breathe

or to spot the release
of his final fluids, crawling
the cold concrete,
in the shape of River Jordan,
while bystanders record videos,
and beg *please*,
> Bro, *you're killing him*

So I set out to put the bluebird box
to rights, but a house sparrow attacks me
and I realize, in this terrible world,
I cannot save even one desperate bluebird,
fluttering before infinity, begging me.

We do well. We feel safe.
We will not live life off target.
Let us bow our heads,
thankful for the fine-grained crust,
the yielding inner crumb.
The wine oaky, sweetened with song
trilled on angel food tongues,
we grow plump as low-hanging fruit.

Out on the street, fallen
while no one was looking,
the nameless siphon sustenance
from their bones, hunched, rootless,
left to sizzle in the skillet,
so many futures fricasseed.

Out on the street children spin
despair's fouled honey.
All our à la mode speeches,
our *but for the grace* quotes, cannot
atone for the bounty uneaten,
tossed into dumpsters at end of day,
our legislators pickling the batter.

Out on the street a fairy godmother,
hell-bent for butter.

Unlike the fables—
cold porridge, toxic apples,
parents left with a sickly
succotash of choice—
she salvages second-day cuisine
via cherry-red hatchback.
Hustles to rewrite stories,
one underpass,
one home delivery,
one meal-sized
biodegradable container
at a time.

—*Christopher C. Davis (1857–1881)*

When silence becomes too heavy
for the heart to carry and ears
know only the unimaginable as tempo,
let these words be a trumpet,
a chorus of circular breaths.

When the past becomes flesh
and the wind whistles shrill, echoed
by a thin whine of branches,
and mockingbirds loose their taunts,
loop and fray with ragged wings.

When history has no scruples,
leaves us only the malice and musk,
the frenzy of boots and torches
and thick braided hemp, noosed, knotted,
South Bridge, Athens County, Ohio,
a blue sheen of moon over the bones.

Oh, how the air cleaves its privilege.

When at last our shame unfurls,
a wretched flag, every frayed thread
uncoiled, we pen our truths,
every word a sepulchre, every syllable
a stone rolled away.

Five

Let the rain in,
let it soak through.

ENDING

In the end, does it really matter
the way anything said in passing
grew so much larger, how we
took on sorrow and stored it
until we stood in silence or wept,

how much we loved, or how
love broke us—how we longed
for a quickening, the crumbling
of right and wrong, to live
in a language free of the splintery
cold of our foolish selves.

The last stars arc, dim the sash.
Wails the pitch of a coal mine's siren
quiver my temporal bone, a song to dig a hole.
My grandfathers, coal caked, muscle
and blood, yoked to Peabody scrip,

sinking shaft or pit, railroad cars tippled,
cinder and soot smutting miles of track,
valley fills steeped in acid spoil,
one hundred years of forest sheared.

Pained as I am to reflect, my great-greats,
pigeon toed, gap mouthed, pondering
how the hard-working find themselves
both proud and begging, held fast,
like a flag that never waves.

Who hasn't rationalized themselves
a noble son or daughter, their life tightly
squeezed between two fists?

Tonight, roaming the ether,
I visit their graves, blush-pink peonies
to decorate each stone. Saying nothing,
I write, one finger in dust,
fire in our hearts, fire in our souls,
forever together, *down in the hole*.

I started out this day elbowing
my grandmother's forget-me-not
teacup off the counter beside the sink.
Sobbed as I swept a million jagged
memories, scattered across the kitchen floor.

Now my feet up, a glass of sweet tea,
I watch birds at the feeder.
A quarrel of house sparrows peck
at the smalls, gorge themselves on seed,
as if they deserve to.

I once told my grandmother a rich man
hurt me. Her bent head told me
to keep that story to myself.
I revisit what it means to be ruined
over and over in my sleep, imagine ways
to dismember him, as if that might help
glue my own broken pieces back together.

Consider daffodil blades
in the crackling cold of February,
those green thumbs-up
breaking through earth's rind,
obliterating doubt—what's left
of winter suddenly endurable.

What tethers us to the tentative,
to contingencies, to the life force
we are designed to abandon from birth?

I am reluctant to call it destiny, knowing
too well which neuroses rush forth
from that word, sifted through lobes
and sockets to lubricate our worry.

Listen—there are things to love
about failure too. Sometimes
we make mistakes, call them coincidence,
trapped like thirsty sponges
between memory and the moment,
our imagined selves the deal we make.

Aren't most of us in fact still children
mishandling oversized bodies,
echoing songs seeded in our mind's eye?

We pump our legs on a playground swing,
avoid the dare to jump, the grass
beneath our feet heeled to death,
the slaughtered ground a pit of sharps
and flats, scars the shape of shattered
hearts stamped into our elbows and knees.

how they work to keep you down,
call you fat, shoeless,
say you have no teeth.

But you got teeth, plenty.
Ask any city man thinking to park
his fracking machines in your valley.
And the earth responds,
rewards you in petals,
herbs, sweet potato vines.

And yes, we know, one good fiddle lick
makes you forget tired or hungry,
and yes, that is your voice,
strong and true, front row of the choir
come Sunday morning, slipping
more than you ought in the donation box,
because you cannot bear to think
of any of your neighbors going without.

Generation to generation,
childhood to womanhood,
failing crops and dying children,
the mine siren's doom.
Your sorrows like echoes
rippling through the holler
and entered with careful cursive
in the family Bible.

So when they call you soft, I say,
You are not soft.
You are limestone.
You are flint.
You are mountain shine,
feed-sack proud.
You are diamond.

I worry over how to dress in this world,
where the shield we are given as a child
does not protect, our cinched belts tugged tight.

Everyone is doing trigger warnings now,
and there are words I've had to step away from,
nights I could not sleep from careless use,

calling out to shadows, as though
impressions at tight right angles
could be woven into reason.

Outside under midnight's glitter burlesque,
coyote music tempers moon's heavy breath.

Sometimes stars draw lines so perfect
they carve my name.

If only there were a heron in this photograph,
silhouetted at a distance in steel-gray dawn,
stilted legs, shaggy plume soaked in stillness,
daggerlike bill bending sound in every direction.
And locust trees, breeze-bobbing by the pond,
clusters of blue flag iris unfurling, a random
spritz of honeysuckle, a nattering bee.

Instead, there is a tightly cropped close-up—
a diary I guarded as a teen, half-buried
in shadow, every word enshrined a scar
embracing its wound, the damp morning grass
the square root of loss, the thickness
of the air suffocating the color from a hapless
monarch's wings.

Curls of bobbing hair and my stick figure
locked inside this catalog, every blemish
and blunder a vividly documented humiliation,
sewn together by scratches of adolescent ink,
an invisible thread of misconceptions forever
twisted taut against my throat, the first blood
of sunrise slinking low on the horizon.

I've pummeled, overfed, starved,
and liquored you up. Squeezed you
into little black dresses, sent you off
in stiletto heels without bail money.
Made fun of you, cursed your
potbelly, saggy underarms, blamed
you for my briggity sense of self.

I confess, I spent most of my childhood
holed up in you, stuffing you with confections,
filling empty spaces labeled *loneliness*
and *afraid*, chubby fingers brushing
crumbs and tears. I'm still belly flopping,
a box of Keebler Chocolate Chunks
stashed in the back of the cupboard.

Well done, hormones. I riled you
at every opportunity, clenched
and unclenched my fists, dredged up
mistakes and injustices in the middle
of the night, your hefty amalgamations
lighting me up, until one day
you about-faced, whipped my ass.

Oh my heart. All those come-hither
man-boys siphoning you dry, your frazzled
chambers filled with flimflam and prattle.

When Daddy died, I thought sure
you would quit me. When is the last time
we laughed so hard we cried?

Bone temple—crepe-husked, cap-toothed,
cockled brow. Who was it said
we can be anything we want to be?
I bend the knee: a pact, a truce,
a clink of glassware—a toast to tenacity,
our snort laughter, the overbite
of our jaw scraping our lower lip.

I spent time today studying
forehead lines, linked into yet another
Zoom meeting, my screen a window
of windows inside a dollhouse.
I like to think I have good ears
and what I hear is this—grateful.
Grateful for technology, poetry,
song, an unusual autumn of sun
and balmy breezes prevailing
well into November, leaves clinging
to their colors like a Matisse painting
or a toddler with a fist of Crayolas.
Time moves, then moves again
and forehead lines are bar charts,
flesh-and-bone diagrams of courage.

Fiddle riffs ricochet bedroom walls.
I yawn, stretch. My husband, in the kitchen,
loads the toaster, cranks the radio,
adds his rich tenor:

Headed down south
to the land of the pine

I run, barefoot and bed-headed, his arms
thrown wide, we *box the gnat*, whirl
alongside kitchen table, living room chairs,
a filched synthetic tulip between his teeth:

Rock me, mama, like a wagon wheel
Rock me, mama, any way you feel

Near the final chorus, he tosses
the tulip, bends me with a flourish.
We dangle, mashing mouths, tongues
in waves, collapse in giggles on the sofa.

Rock me, mama, like a southbound train
Hey, mama, rock me

Strolling back to the kitchen,
my husband eats cold toast,
wearing only his socks.

The silvery shiver of a lone flute, as condolers arrive.
My husband's ex-wife plays a mean one, so hire her,
which will unquestionably raise some eyebrows.
Someone must dress as a young Gloria Steinem,
fist-pumping feminist, another as Lieutenant Uhura,
feisty Science Goddess of interstellar communiqué.
Bright colors, tie-dyed or paisley, extra points
for those who braid their hair or beards.
Arrange pillows in a circle, and inside the circle
a fountain of dark chocolate, a cauldron
of melted Gruyère, an assortment of four-letter words
and shortbreads for fondueing. Hang a hammock,
scatter prayer rugs, burn incense, a bit of mugwort
to call the spirits. Light a candle, read James Wright.
Break out the Springsteen, the kegs and Jell-O shots.
I want blue plastic wading pools and bare feet,
a group sing-along—ABBA, the Eagles, Blue Öyster Cult.
Pass a joint, hold up Bic lighters, talk my son
into recounting stories of my tofu flimflammeries.
Don't let my second husband sit in a corner by himself
or my first bogart the doobie. The eulogies should be short,
the piñata stuffed with neologisms and the wide, wide reach
of love, more than enough to fill vast and trackless spaces.

ACKNOWLEDGMENTS

Grateful acknowledgment is made to the editors of these journals, in which several of the poems first appeared, some slightly altered.

Anti-Heroin Chic: "Cousin"
Change Seven: "Say His Name," "To Those Messaging Me after My Mother's Passing"
Chiron Review: "Buzz Whitedog"
Cutleaf: "I Look for My Dead Mother in New York," "Subsequently Hereafter," "To Save a Life"
Delta Poetry Review: "You Know the Story"
Green Mountain Review: "Outside Her Window," "River's Way"
Gyroscope Review: "Ten O'clock, the Day Already Threatening"
Heartwood: "The Trouble with Apples"
New Ohio Review: "Vernal Equinox"
New York Times: "By All Indications"
One: "Rare Birds"
ONE ART: "Because Coal," "Because Autumn Always Clotheslines Me," "Bone Thin," "Power Out on the Mountain," "The Softening," "Tennessee Homeland"
Pine Mountain Sand & Gravel: "An Appalachian Woman's Guide to Beer Drinking"
Rattle: "The Whole Shebang up for Debate"
Red Earth Review: "Girls of Summer"
Rise Up Review: "Illumination"
Sheila-Na-Gig: "Alone in the House of My Heart," "Badasses," "Hella Barbie 1968," "Leftovers"
Sky Island Journal: "Bobcat," "Obituary"
Stirring: "Weather Report"
SWWIM: "The House, the Barn, the Sheep, the Chickens"
The American Journal of Poetry: "Oh You Woman of Appalachia"

Thimble: "After the Fire"
Twelve Mile Review: "Totemic Sponsors"
Vine Leaves Literary Journal: "Splintered"

"Bad Blood" was published in *Riparian*, ed. Sherry Cook Stanforth and Richard Hague (Dos Madres, 2019).

"Sense of One's Place" and "Ohio Struggles to Contain COVID-19 Nursing Home Deaths" were published in *Anthology of Appalachian Writers*, ed. Sylvia Bailey Shurbutt, vols. 12 and 13 (Sheridan Books, 2020 and 2021).

"To No One in Particular" was published in *Aeolian Harp*, ed. Megan Merchant and Ami Kaye, vol. 7 (Glass Lyre, 2021).

"An Appalachian Woman's Guide to Beer Drinking" was republished in *Norwegian Writers' Climate Campaign* (2021). https://forfatternesklimaaksjon.no/in-english/.

"Badasses" was republished in *Pine Mountain Sand & Gravel*, ed. Sherry Cook Stanforth, vol. 24 (Dos Madres, 2021).

"Leftovers" was republished in *Poetry X Hunger*, November 11, 2020.

"Splintered" was republished in *Mason Street Literary Magazine*, Fall 2021.

"Splintered," "Ten O'clock, the Day Already Threatening," and "Weather Report" appeared in *Serving*, a chapbook (Crisis Chronicles, 2018).

"To Save a Life" (originally published as "Saving Sgt. Billings") won the 2021 Lascaux Prize in Poetry and the 2022 New Ohio Review/Movable Project writing contest.

Kari Gunter-Seymour is the poet laureate of Ohio. She is a recipient of a 2021 Academy of American Poets Laureate Fellowship. Her previous collections are *A Place So Deep Inside America It Can't Be Seen* (Sheila-Na-Gig Editions, 2020), which won the 2020 Ohio Poet of the Year Award, and the chapbook *Serving* (Crisis Chronicles, 2018). Her poems have appeared in numerous journals and publications, including *Rattle, One, New Ohio Review,* and the *New York Times*. Her work has also been featured on *Verse Daily, Cultural Daily, World Literature Today,* and *Poem-a-Day*. A ninth-generation Appalachian, she is the founder/executive director of the Women of Appalachia Project (WOAP) and editor of *Women Speak,* the WOAP anthology series, and of *I Thought I Heard A Cardinal Sing: Ohio's Appalachian Voices,* a one-of-a-kind anthology funded by the Academy of American Poets and the Andrew W. Mellon Foundation. She is the founder, curator, and host of Spoken & Heard, a seasonal performance series featuring poets, writers, and musicians from across the country; an artist in residence at the Wexner Center for the Arts; and a 2021–22 Pillars of Prosperity Fellow for the Foundation for Appalachian Ohio.

www.karigunterseymourpoet.com
@KGunterSeymour